WHEN I GRADUATE,
I WANT TO BE...

The 10-Step Career Planning Journal

Karleen Tauszik

TIP
TOP
BOOKS

Published by Tip Top Books, Dunedin, Florida

Text and layout copyright © 2020 by Karleen Tauszik
Cover Illustration from BigstockPhoto.com, contributor AV Bitter
Cover Design Copyright © 2020 by Karleen Tauszik
Original cover design and cover photo editing by Janet Tauszik

Summary: This journal provides teens and young adults from ages 16 to 22 with a ten-step process to examine their talents, achievements and past job and volunteer experiences to better equip them for career planning and decision making.

ISBN: 978-0-9904899-6-2

Karleen Tauszik is an author, primarily of books for children ages 8-12. She has worked in Human Resources for over 15 years and she's passionate about helping people find the work they were meant to do. Visit her on the web at KarleenT.com, where you can see her other books and sign up for her newsletter.

*If you don't know where you are going,
you'll end up someplace else.*

--YOGI BERRA

Do you dream of being independent but you wonder how you'll make a living? Do you feel pressured by your parents or guidance counselor into focusing on a "sensible" career that sounds boring and uninspiring? Are you wondering what talents you have that you can actually get paid for? Do you constantly wish you could pursue a line of work that others are calling impractical or foolish? If you're in any of these situations, this book is for you.

You're not alone. Most people, regardless of their age, aren't sure what their true talents are and how those talents can be applied to a job. The result? Study after study shows that over 50% of Americans are dissatisfied or even disengaged at their workplace. You run into these people every day. You might be living with a parent or know another family member in that situation.

That's why I wrote this book. With over fifteen years of Human Resources experience, I realize the need for people to be working in jobs that match their true strengths and talents. That's where they'll most likely enjoy their work, do their best, and excel.

"But I don't know my true strengths and talents," you might say. In this ten-step journal, you'll discover them. First, we'll explore your present situation—the reasons you're reading this book and what you want to achieve. Then we'll look back at the talents and interests you've had throughout your life. From there, we'll plan your future and look at how to apply your unique skills and talents to your career decisions.

Working on one section a week, in just ten weeks you'll have a clearer direction for your next steps. And in the future, keep this book handy, refer back to it, and add memories, experiences, and insights as they come to you. There are several pages at the end to record additional notes and ideas.

Whether you're in the last couple years of high school, planning to go straight to work after graduation, almost done with college, or planning on the military, vo-tech training, or an apprenticeship in a trade, use *When I Graduate, I Want To Be...* as your roadmap for career satisfaction and success.

Table of Contents

1. My Present Situation

Before we explore the potential direction of your career, let's assess your current situation.

The current date is _____ and you're using this book because

_____

_____

_____

When you look ahead ten years at your ideal career situation, what do you think or feel about your prospects?_____

_____

_____

_____

_____

How do your current plans (or lack of plans) make you feel?_____

_____

_____

_____

Are there factors about your future that make you uneasy? What are they?_____

_____

_____

_____

What things do you like about your current life? _____

_____

_____

_____

_____

What do you dislike about your life? Are those aspects changeable? _____

_____

_____

_____

_____

What are your current hobbies? _____

_____

_____

What have you always wanted to learn more about? _____

_____

_____

What do you wish you could do in your ideal career? _____

_____

_____

Other thoughts and insights about your career plans and potential at this point:

_____

_____

2. Looking Back to Ages 6 to 10

Looking back can help you move forward. It can provide insights into yourself which may have gotten buried over the years.

If you have a hard time recalling some of these childhood memories, try asking your siblings, your parents, close relatives, and childhood friends. For more help jogging your memory, look at old schoolwork, report cards, family photos, and other memorabilia you and your parents kept from your childhood.

When adults asked you, "What do you want to be when you grow up?", what was your usual answer? _____

_____

As a child, what were your favorite books usually about? _____

_____

_____

What were your favorite classes in elementary school? _____

_____

_____

What were your favorite collections and hobbies? _____

_____

_____

When you had free time, what did you like to do? _____

_____

_____

What was your favorite family vacation? Why? _____

_____

_____

When you were little, you were known as the kid who always _____

_____

_____

In your elementary school years, what was your proudest moment? _____

_____

_____

What were your top three talents or strengths during this period? _____

_____

_____

Additional memories that may be relevant are _____

_____

_____

_____

_____

_____

_____

_____

_____

3. Looking Back to Ages 11 to 15

This is an important time to explore because once you hit adolescence, chances are you started to get pulled away from your inborn strengths and talents. First, peer pressure was probably strong in pushing you away from childish things and toward adulthood. That's normal and needed, but some of those childish things may have been keys to your future career success.

Also, during these years you become more aware of societal expectations and may have started to get pulled off track by well-meaning guidance counselors, teachers, mentors, and even your parents.

When you were in middle school and the first years of high school what career did you think you wanted to pursue? _____

_____

_____

What were your favorite classes? Why? _____

_____

_____

Did you have a collection or a hobby during these years? What was it? Why did you take it up? _____

_____

_____

When you had free time, what did you like to do? _____

_____

_____

What did friends or family turn to you for help with?

_____

_____

What extra-curricular activities were you involved in? Did you enjoy them, or were they forced upon you? _____

_____

_____

When you had to break into teams for a project at school, what role did you usually end up with? □ the leader □ the note taker □ the presenter □ the idea person

Why? _____

_____

_____

Did you like working with others, or prefer solo projects? _____

_____

During these years, what was your proudest accomplishment? _____

_____

_____

What was an event that really excited you? Why? _____

_____

_____

_____

How do the answers in this section compare to your answers from ages 6 to 10? What changed? _____

_____

_____

_____

Did you start getting pushed or pulled in a certain career direction during these years? How and by whom? Into what career possibilities? _____

_____

_____

_____

_____

Did you agree with this career direction? Why or why not? _____

_____

_____

_____

From age 11 to 15, what did you think your ideal future life looked like? _____

_____

_____

_____

_____

Did you work, have chores, or volunteer anywhere when you were old enough? List these. How did you get them? What parts were interesting or boring?

Additional memories that may be relevant are

4. Ages 16 to 22

During these pivotal years, you likely feel pressure to make the "right" career decisions. Whether you go straight to full-time work after high school, pursue training for a trade, join the military, or go to college, these years start putting you more on track for the future. Pick the path you took (or are planning to take)—college, vo-tech training/military, or straight into a job.

Since this book is for ages 16 to 22, each question is presented for the full age range: future focused "will you" questions for those who are still in high school, and past focused "did you" questions for those who have moved beyond high school. Answer the questions that apply to your situation.

Will you probably go to college? What do you think your major will be? Why? **OR** Did you go to college? What was your major? Why did you pick it? What were your favorite classes? Were they in your major? _____

_____

_____

_____

_____

_____

Will you probably go to vo-tech school, the military, or an apprenticeship in a trade? In what area? Why that area? **OR** Did you pursue technical training, the military, or an apprenticeship in a trade? In what area? Why did you pick it? Did you enjoy the training? If so, what was your favorite part? If not, what did you dislike? _____

_____

_____

Will you probably go straight into full-time work after high school? What type of job do you think you'll get? Why? **OR** Did you go straight into full-time work after high school? In what area? Why did you pick it? Did you enjoy the job? If so, what was your favorite part? If not, what did you dislike?

If you could go back in time and decide over again, would you pick a different path? What would it be? _____

Recently, what have you been happy about completing? _____

What activity gives you energy or makes you lose track of time? _____

If you were to win first prize for anything right now, what would it be?

_____

_____

You can't pass up a book or article about _____

_____

What person would you like to spend the day with? (This can be a historical or fictitious character.) Why that person? _____

_____

_____

Friends and family tend to turn to you when they need help with _____

_____

_____

If you worked during these years, list the jobs you held. Include volunteer assignments too. List the company or organization name and the role you had, and answer these questions: How did you get the job? Why did you pursue that particular opportunity? What parts were interesting or boring? How long did you stay? Why did you leave? Was the location convenient? How were the hours? Did you like the environment? And finally, who was your boss and what did you like or dislike about him or her? Did the experience give you any insight (positive or negative) to what you wanted for your future career? _____

_____

_____

_____

5. Your History to the Present

You have unique strengths, but you might not be able to recognize them. After all, you've been living with them all these years and you might think they're common among most people. This section will help to highlight your superpowers.

Look back at pages 5 through 12 for ages 6 to 15. What did you want to be during those phases?

From age 6 to 10: ....

From age 11 to 15: ....

Summarize your strengths and achievements from those younger years. Do you still feel strong in those areas? Why or why not? ....

....

....

....

....

....

What do you think have been your greatest achievements to date? ....

....

....

....

....

....

....

Looking over your job and volunteering history on pages 15 through 17, what have been your smartest career decisions? _____

_____

_____

Ask at least five other people individually about what they see as your strengths. List the person's name and response. _____

_____

_____

_____

_____

_____

_____

_____

_____

Now that you've answered these questions, what three words would you use to describe yourself? 1. _____ 2. _____

3. _____

In your opinion, your top positive attributes are _____

_____

_____

Have those attributes been used in any of your job, school, or volunteer situations so far? How? _____

_____

_____

_____

_____

_____

_____

_____

_____

Read through what you've entered into this book, going back to age 6. As you review each page, add any additional notes that come to mind. You might want to highlight some things that stand out to you. Look for some common threads of what you liked and what you didn't like. Insights like that will help you make better decisions going forward. Summarize what stands out for you. _____

_____

_____

_____

_____

_____

_____

_____

_____

_____

_____

_____

6. What You History Tells You

What have you learned about yourself? How does it line up with the plans and dreams you have for your future? _____

_____

_____

_____

_____

_____

_____

Looking back at your work and/or volunteer experience, what are the top four or five things that made you happy at work? _____

_____

_____

How many of those elements will likely be present in your future career? Which ones? _____

_____

_____

Rate your bosses. Look back on pages 15 through 17 and pick your top favorite 2 and your least favorite 2 (if you've had that many).

Top 2: _____

Bottom 2: _____

Are there any common threads with the top 2 or the bottom 2? Why did you pick each one for that ranking? Knowing this will help you when you meet potential bosses in job interviews.

Think about the people you worked with at each job. Did you have to work as a team or alone? What was your preference? Are you still friends with any of those people?

Which jobs or projects made time fly?

Were you promoted at any of your jobs? Was that a good thing, or were the new responsibilities too difficult?

Did you receive any awards or achievement recognition at any of the jobs or in school? For what? _____

_____

_____

_____

Were any of your duties in line with the top three talents and strengths you listed on page 6, your childhood strengths? _____

_____

_____

Additional things you noticed and want to note: _____

_____

_____

_____

_____

_____

_____

_____

_____

_____

_____

_____

_____

7. Finding Your Ikigai

Ikigai is a Japanese word that means, "a reason for living". According to this method, if you consider the factors that make life worthwhile—passion, mission, vocation, and profession—and find a path of work where all four overlap, you have found your best source of purpose and satisfaction in your work.

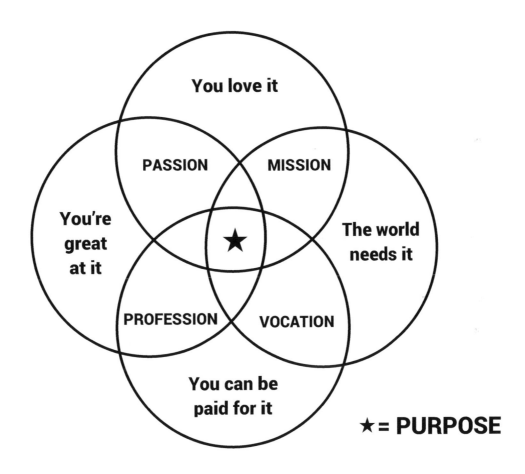

As you can see from this illustration, your **mission** is the intersection of what you love and what the world needs. Your **vocation** is the intersection of what the world needs and what you can be paid for. Your **profession** is the intersection of what you do well and what you can be paid for. And your **passion** is at the intersection of what you do well and what you love to do. Finally, your **purpose** is at the intersection of all four circles.

If you can find something you love, which you are good at, which the world needs, and for which you can be paid, you've found your ideal direction for life, a direction that's a balance between the four forces. Working through this can give you clarity on your ideal job.

Take time over the next week to slow down and think about the answers to the questions in the four sections. Write whatever answers come to mind. Try this for several days in a row, coming back to the questions and adding any new ideas.

Things you can do that you love:

_____

_____

_____

_____

Things you can do that the world needs:

_____

_____

_____

_____

Things you can do which you can be paid for:

_____

_____

_____

_____

Things you can do that you're especially good at: _____

_____

_____

_____

After you've pondered these questions for a few days, highlight the top things you resonate with in the four sections and fill them in here:

You love _____

_____

The world needs _____

_____

You can get paid for _____

_____

You're great at _____

_____

Have you found anything in your lists that is the same for all four sections? _____

_____

Or have you found something that's the same in only three sections? Is there a way to make it four? _____

_____

For example, if accounting is what you're good at, is what you can get paid for, and is something the world needs, is there a way it can bring you joy? What if you work as an accountant for a non-profit that interests you? Or what if you started your own accounting business?

Or if you love drawing cartoons and you're good at it, but you think no one will pay you for it, is that true? There are others in the world getting paid for cartoons. How are they doing it? Can you research to find out? Can you try taking a few hours a week to try to sell your work and see what happens?

Look back at your interests from ages 6 to 15 on pages 5 through 12. Do you see new ways you can nurture some of those earlier interests? _____

_____

_____

Look back as page 23 at the four or five things that make you happy at work. How many of them can be incorporated into your ideal job? How can you integrate them?_____

_____

_____

_____

Additional things you noticed and want to note: _____

_____

_____

_____

8. Your Ideal Life

In this section, throw aside your reality and dream big. Think about your life in an ideal world. You just may find some nuggets here that can actually be incorporated into your next career steps.

Your big dream is

_____

_____

_____

_____

Your smaller dreams are

_____

_____

_____

_____

The job you always thought you'd love is: _____

_____

If you had an extra hour of free time, how would you spend it? What about a week of free time?

_____

_____

_____

If you were going to start a business, it would be _____

_____

_____

What would you do if you had enough money that you didn't have to work?

_____

_____

_____

Describe a day in the life of your ideal dream life. Where do you live? Where do you work? What type of work do you do? What do you do in your spare time? What type of people do you hang out with? Include any other details that are important to you. _____

_____

_____

_____

_____

_____

_____

_____

_____

_____

_____

_____

9. Your Influencers

Throughout this book, you've been discovering what you do well and what matters to you in terms of your work life. This planning and thinking can help you make an informed choice when picking from the thousands of options that are available.

But at this point, you might be wondering how your ideal life from the previous chapter will go over with your parents, guidance counselor, or other influencers who are in your life. As you start sharing your hopes and plans, you need to be careful to understand the perspective of people who may want to squash your dreams.

Let's start with parents. They love you and usually want what they feel will be best for you: a secure future with a good job. Some parents focus on how much you can make vs. your happiness in the job. It's likely that they've had their own patches of financial struggles and want to shield you from those experiences. Fair enough. It's important to understand their perspective as you enter into these discussions.

People in your situation usually make career choices in one of two ways:

1) They pick something because they think it will lead to something else, whether they enjoy it or not. This usually doesn't work out well. You can't predict the future—it's too complicated and unpredictable. And once you start getting a steady paycheck in a career that's not ideal for you, it's easy to get stuck here, especially as you take on expenses of life: a car payment, rent or a mortgage, a family, and so on.

OR

2) They choose a path they think will be valuable, whether it leads to something better or not. They pick something interesting where their strengths and interests can be used. If they need to scrimp on expenses for awhile until they can

gain a foothold in their career, they do so happily because they're doing work they love and they're willing to sacrifice as they practice and learn to become more valuable in that job market. Through this scenario, they might fail often, but they learn and improve from each failure.

Guess which of those two choices usually have the best outcome in career success and happiness? Guess which one was followed by most of the famous CEOs, artists, musicians, athletes, actors, and business people who are at the top of their fields? Option 2 is the winner. That said, option 2 takes a focused commitment for the long term. That means continually learning about the field, practicing perseverance, and climbing the ladder one rung at a time.

Because they love you, parents and influencers will usually try to steer you toward "something you can fall back on", a "reliable" career that has plenty of job openings. Understand this perspective, but realize that you'll need to make a strong case for your own ideal career ideas. Be ready to answer their concerns of how you'll survive and present them with the details from this book on how you think you'll work that out.

The important thing is to focus on your strengths, not on trying to make your weaknesses stronger. Try to avoid career decisions that will force you to improve what you know you're not good at. Instead, always keep your strengths in mind.

What do you think your parents and/or influencers will think of your career plans?

You'll need to find a balance between career fantasies, reality, and the possibilities you want to pursue. What evidence can you provide them that your plans are a good idea? What success have you had that supports your plans? How have you already shown dedication and perseverance in learning and growing toward expertise in your target career area?

How can you address what you predict will be their most pressing objections?

10. Your Career Plan

Congratulations! You've learned quite a bit about yourself and your future career potential by working through these 9 sections. Now it's time to set some goals for the next steps in your career path.

Over these past 9 chapters, what were the top things you learned? _____

_____

_____

_____

Your ideal job is _____

_____

Now set a target goal. You can't hit a target you can't see. Take an inventory. Who do you need to contact to talk about this plan? Maybe you need do some research or contact some industry experts to determine your next steps. Your goal is to

_____

_____

_____

A reasonable deadline is _____ .

It's important to get started while these ideas are fresh, even if it means you only take small steps. At least they'll be steps in the right direction. Remember, there's never a "perfect" time, so start now. As you start moving toward your goal, you'll gain momentum. Plus, you'll show your influencers that you're serious about your plans and you're willing to put in the work needed to achieve them.

Some steps you can take immediately are

Your action steps over this month will be

Looking ahead, your action steps next month will be

Steps you'll need to take into the future will be

Do you foresee some obstacles? Make a list of them here, along with ideas of how to deal with them.

Good luck on your journey to career satisfaction. Now that you know where you're going, you'll be able to more effectively map out how to get there. Keep this book handy as your guide, and you'll soon be sharing your best strengths with the world!

--- Notes & Ideas ---

--- Notes & Ideas ---

--- Notes & Ideas ---

--- Notes & Ideas ---

About the Author

Karleen Tauszik is the author of over 20 books. Most of them are for children ages 8 to 12. She created the popular career possibility journal for children, *When I Grow Up, I Want to Be...* and after hearing many adults say, "When are you going to write the book for adults?", she created another book, *In My Next Job, I Want to Be...* and this one, *When I Graduate, I Want to Be...* for ages 16 to 22.

To cover all ages, Karleen plans to add one more book to the *I Want to Be* series in 2020, releasing *When I Retire, I Want to Be...* for those who are 55+ and want to pursue new endeavors.

Learn more by visiting Karleen's website at KarleenT.com. While you're there, keep up to date with her news and book releases by signing up for her newsletter.

Made in the USA
Columbia, SC
08 October 2021